R.E.A.D. I.T.

hom E
dA ily
recor D

I ncluding
T ips and awards

HOME
READING

Middle Level

Name: ....

Teacher: ....

Grade: .... **Year:** ....

School: ....

Written by Stan Kluzek & Andrew Coldwell

Kluwell Publications

R.E.A.D. I.T. Home Reading - Middle Level
ISBN 0-9585742-5-1

First published in 1996 by
Kluwell Publications
P.O. Box 55, Strathdale, Victoria, Australia 3550
Phone: 61-3-54411379
email: info@kluwell.com
Web Site: www.kluwell.com

U.S. Edition 2003

Acknowledgements:
Graphics used by permission of Gary Clark, Swamp Productions P/L
Cover design by Stephen Brown

Printed by Mulqueen Printers, Bendigo

Using this Book

This book is designed to be used by both the parent(s) and the student.

HOME READING

Comments

A brief comment is required each night your child has been reading. This comment can be written by either your child or yourself.

If your child does not read **DO NOT** write a comment, that is leave that night blank.

Some **examples** of comments are:-
- I loved the plot.
- I couldn't stop reading!
- Read a lot tonight.
- I love books by this author.
- It was scary...............
- Easy to read.
- It was funny when ....
- I didn't enjoy this book.
- The ending was different to what I expected.
- My favorite character was / is ....

PARENTS please sign your initials after each comment!

3

Date & Title	Comment	😊 😐 😟	Number of Days
Mon /			
Tues /			
Wed /			
Thur /			
Fri /			
Comment			

Date / /

Date & Title	Comment	😊 😐 😟	Number of Days
Mon /			
Tues /			
Wed /			
Thur /			
Fri /			
Comment			

Date / /

FOR YOUR CHILD TO DO

Your child has the opportunity to show what they felt about the reading they have done by giving the faces a smile, frown or just a straight line for the mouth.

Don't forget to KEEP COUNT of the NUMBER OF DAYS that reading has taken place (to be shown in the right hand column).

Older children do not have to be heard, but could have the TIME spent reading recorded e.g. 30 minutes

15 minutes

The PAGES read should be recorded if the material takes more than a night to read.

The RESPONSIBILITY for writing the comment could be left with the child.

The idea of this book is that it should be used as a record of what is read during the week (Mon - Fri). It is a record of the number of nights reading occurs, not the number of books read.

Although we realize that reading is done during the weekend, part of the idea of this book is to form good reading habits during the week. (FRIDAY NIGHT COULD BE DONE OVER THE WEEKEND.)

Date & Title	Comment	☺ ☺ ☺	Number of Days
Mon /			
Tues /			
Wed /			
Thur /			
Fri /			
Comment			

Date   /   /

Date & Title	Comment		
Mon /			
Tues /			
Wed /			
Thur /			
Fri /			
Comment			

Date   /   /

When reading a book you could discuss the following statements:-

I enjoyed reading this book.

Strongly agree | Agree | Disagree | Strongly disagree

I would like to read more books by this author.

Strongly agree | Agree | Disagree | Strongly disagree

I could think of a friend that would like to read this book.

Strongly agree | Agree | Disagree | Strongly disagree

This book would also be suitable for adults to read.

Strongly agree | Agree | Disagree | Strongly disagree

This book is suitable for both boys and girls.

Strongly agree | Agree | Disagree | Strongly disagree

Date & Title	Comment	😊 😐 😞	Number of Days
Mon /			
Tues /			
Wed /			
Thur /			
Fri /			
Comment			
		Date /	/
Mon /			
Tues /			
Wed /			
Thur /			
Fri /			
Comment			
		Date /	/

Reading Award

CONGRATULATIONS!
This is the FIRST of many
awards for the year.

AWARDED TO

....

FOR
25 NIGHTS READING

Signed ....

DATE: /   /

Date & Title	Comment	😊 😐 😞	Number of Days
Mon /			
Tues /			
Wed /			
Thur /			
Fri /			

Comment

Date / /

Date & Title	Comment	😊 😐 😞	Number of Days
Mon /			
Tues /			
Wed /			
Thur /			
Fri /			

Comment

Date / /

A Suitable Reading Environment should be :-

* Quiet.

* Comfortable.

* Where you can be close to your child.

* Relaxing for both you and your child.

* Free from interruptions.

* Enjoyable, interesting and passionate.

* Full of opportunities to praise your child.

FLIT FLAP
FLAPFLIT
FLIT

REMEMBER to be seen as a **READER YOURSELF**

Date & Title	Comment	😊 😐 🙁	Number of Days
Mon /			
Tues /			
Wed /			
Thur /			
Fri /			

Comment

Date / /

Date & Title	Comment	😊 😐 🙁	Number of Days
Mon /			
Tues /			
Wed /			
Thur /			
Fri /			

Comment

Date / /

Reading Award

Swooping in on your 2nd Award.

WELL DONE!

AWARDED TO

FOR
50 NIGHTS READING

Signed

DATE: /   /

Date & Title	Comment	☺ ☻ ☹	Number of Days
Mon /			
Tues /			
Wed /			
Thur /			
Fri /			
Comment			
		Date / /	
Mon /			
Tues /			
Wed /			
Thur /			
Fri /			
Comment			
		Date / /	

14

BE
PATIENT

Do encourage your child to guess what the story is about.

Do praise your child when an idea or word is used that you know will come up in the story.

Do ask questions like:-

"What can you tell about the story from the picture?"

"What do you think will happen in the story?"

Do talk about the start of the story, what happened by the end of the story, the people in the story....etc.

Do mention things like:-

The person who wrote the story - *the author.*

The person who did the illustrations - *the illustrator.*

Find these people on the front cover of the book. Where else can you find their names?

Do make sure that whatever your child reads is a complete story, chapter, or thought.

Date & Title	Comment	☺ ☺ ☹	Number of Days
Mon /			
Tues /			
Wed /			
Thur /			
Fri /			

Comment

Date   /   /

Date & Title	Comment	☺ ☺ ☹	Number of Days
Mon /			
Tues /			
Wed /			
Thur /			
Fri /			

Comment

Date   /   /

ONE WAY OF HELPING YOUR CHILD UNDERSTAND WHAT THEY ARE READING OR LISTENING TO, IS TO GET YOUR CHILD TO ASK QUESTIONS.

SUGGESTIONS TO HELP INCREASE UNDERSTANDING

So .... when you are involved with reading with your child try the following:-

1. Before reading takes place ask your child to think of one question to ask.
2. The child listens or reads (silently or out loud) thinking about a good question to ask.
3. When reading is finished the child asks their question.
4. You could also ask a question of your child.
5. As your child's questions become more complex you could gradually get them to ask more than one question.

THIS CERTAINLY HELPS WITH UNDERSTANDING WHAT IS READ.

Date & Title	Comment	☺ ☺ ☹	Number of Days
Mon /			
Tues /			
Wed /			
Thur /			
Fri /			
Comment			
		Date / /	
Mon /			
Tues /			
Wed /			
Thur /			
Fri /			
Comment			
		Date / /	

18

READING AWARD

75 Nights Reading is a great achievement

READ ON ...

AWARDED TO

FOR
75 NIGHTS READING

Signed ....

DATE: /   /

Date & Title	Comment	☺ ☺ ☹	Number of Days
Mon /			
Tues /			
Wed /			
Thur /			
Fri /			

Comment

Date / /

Date & Title	Comment		
Mon /			
Tues /			
Wed /			
Thur /			
Fri /			

Comment

Date / /

Does Your Child Do Any Of The Following?

Tick off

☐   Recognize base words within other words.

☐   Name basic parts of a book.

☐   Select own books to read.

☐   Read silently.

☐   Read often.

☐   Show enthusiasm about what they have read.

☐   Read in preference to watching television.

☐   Show interest in what older people are reading. e.g. brothers, sisters, parents.

☐   Read a book as a result of seeing a show about the same topic on television.

Date & Title	Comment	😊 😐 😟	Number of Days
Mon /			
Tues /			
Wed /			
Thur /			
Fri /			

Comment

Date   /   /

Date & Title	Comment	😊 😐 😟	Number of Days
Mon /			
Tues /			
Wed /			
Thur /			
Fri /			

Comment

Date   /   /

READING AWARD

AWARDED TO

....

FOR
100 NIGHTS READING

Signed ....

DATE: / /

Date & Title	Comment	😊 😐 ☹	Number of Days
Mon /			
Tues /			
Wed /			
Thur /			
Fri /			

Comment

Date / /

Date & Title	Comment		
Mon /			
Tues /			
Wed /			
Thur /			
Fri /			

Comment

Date / /

24

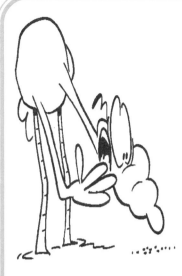

ENCOURAGEMENT
It's so important, but easily overlooked.

ENCOURAGING YOUR CHILD IS ONE OF THE MOST IMPORTANT THINGS YOU CAN DO!

Examples like the following could be used:-

* You worked very hard on that word!
* That was fun.
* Great idea!
* You really seemed to enjoy reading that.
* I can tell you are pleased with your reading.
* That's a tricky word, but I'm sure you can work it out.
* Knowing you, I'm sure you'll be able to choose something to read.
* You're improving in ....
* Look at the progress you have made: .... (tell how)
* I really appreciated you being ready for reading.
* Since you're not happy, what do you think you can do so you'll feel happier?

Date & Title	Comment	☺ ☺ ☹	Number of Days
Mon /			
Tues /			
Wed /			
Thur /			
Fri /			

Comment

Date   /   /

Date & Title	Comment	☺ ☺ ☹	Number of Days
Mon /			
Tues /			
Wed /			
Thur /			
Fri /			

Comment

Date   /   /

CORRECTING MISTAKES YOUR CHILDREN MAKE

☆ If the mistake makes sense, as in a misreading of **home** for **house,** let the child continue to the end of the sentence, then go back and ask. "What word is that?"

☆ If the mistake does not make sense, lead the child to correct the mistake by allowing time to self correct.

☆ Reread what the child has said and ask "Does that make sense?"

☆ Finally, if the meaning is still not clear, look at the word and find familiar sounds such as '*s*' at the beginning and '*ing*' at the end.

Date & Title	Comment	😊 😐 😞	Number of Days
Mon /			
Tues /			
Wed /			
Thur /			
Fri /			
Comment			
		Date / /	
Mon /			
Tues /			
Wed /			
Thur /			
Fri /			
Comment			
		Date / /	

28

READING AWARD

LOOK!
125 Nights Reading

AWARDED TO

....

FOR
125 NIGHTS READING

Signed ....

DATE: / /

Date & Title	Comment	☺ ☺ ☹	Number of Days
Mon /			
Tues /			
Wed /			
Thur /			
Fri /			
Comment Date / /			
Mon /			
Tues /			
Wed /			
Thur /			
Fri /			
Comment Date / /			

(100 - 200 MOST USED WORDS)

again	ever	long	off	told
also	every	look	oh	took
always	father	made	old	two
another	finally	make	only	wanted
any	find	many	other	water
asked	first	money	play	way
away	found	moon	ran	went
bed	friend	more	really	where
before	friends	morning	red	while
best	fun	most	right	white
boy	going	Mr.	room	why
brother	good	Mrs.	say	wish
called	has	much	should	work
children	heard	mom	something	world
Christmas	help	name	started	year
color	here	never	take	years
couldn't	I'd	new	tell	
dad	I'll	next	that's	
dog	I'm	nice	thing	
door	it's	night	thought	
eat	left	now	three	

Date & Title	Comment	☺ ☺ ☹	Number of Days
Mon /			
Tues /			
Wed /			
Thur /			
Fri /			
Comment		Date / /	
Mon /			
Tues /			
Wed /			
Thur /			
Fri /			
Comment		Date / /	

AWARDED TO

....

FOR
150 NIGHTS READING

Signed

....

DATE: /   /

Date & Title	*Comment*	😊 😐 😞	Number of Days
Mon /			
Tues /			
Wed /			
Thur /			
Fri /			

Comment

Date / /

Mon /			
Tues /			
Wed /			
Thur /			
Fri /			

Comment

Date / /

Reading tips for Parents

Praise every effort in reading, especially if your child's confidence is low. Don't compare a child's performance with that of friends or relatives.

Involve the child in the selection of a story or a book.

Ask your child to tell you about something that interests him/her. Use this information when selecting reading material for your child.

Draw out as much information as you can.

We as adults seldom read something that we don't want to so why force young children to read something they are not interested in!

This is not to say that there is not a time and place for compulsory selection and reading of books.

You must balance that yourself.

Date & Title	Comment	☺ ☺ ☺	Number of Days
Mon /			
Tues /			
Wed /			
Thur /			
Fri /			

Comment

Date / /

Date & Title	Comment	☺ ☺ ☺	Number of Days
Mon /			
Tues /			
Wed /			
Thur /			
Fri /			

Comment

Date / /

READING AWARD

AWARDED TO

FOR
175 NIGHTS READING

Signed

DATE: /   /

Date & Title	Comment	😊 😐 😞	Number of Days
Mon /			
Tues /			
Wed /			
Thur /			
Fri /			
Comment			
		Date / /	
Mon /			
Tues /			
Wed /			
Thur /			
Fri /			
Comment			
		Date / /	

CHILDREN COULD BE ASKED ANY OF THE FOLLOWING QUESTIONS WHEN THEY HAVE FINISHED READING A BOOK:

* Did you enjoy the book? Why?
* How did you choose it?
* Was the book boring? Why?
* Who were the characters?
    - Which was your favorite
    - How could you describe this character?
* How long did it take you to read?
* Was there anything about it you
   did not like?
* Could you read your favorite piece?
* Are you going to read any more books by the
   same author?
* Could you make a better ending?
* Did you come
across any unusual
words or words you
did not know the
meaning of?
* Can you give a
brief description of
what happened in
the story?

Date & Title	Comment	😊 😐 ☹	Number of Days
Mon /			
Tues /			
Wed /			
Thur /			
Fri /			
Comment			
		Date / /	
Mon /			
Tues /			
Wed /			
Thur /			
Fri /			
Comment			
		Date / /	

What to read?

Don't restrict your child's reading materials to only books. Provide the chance to read other types of reading material such as:-

Magazines
Comics
Poetry books
Newspapers
Diaries
Reference materials
Atlases
Maps (road maps, street directories)
Instructions for games, machines, etc.
Cooking recipes
Computer Adventure Games
Letters
Telephone Book

Encourage a particular interest by talking and continued reading.

Date & Title	Comment	☺ ☺ ☹	Number of Days
Mon /			
Tues /			
Wed /			
Thur /			
Fri /			

Comment

Date / /

Date & Title	Comment	☺ ☺ ☹	Number of Days
Mon /			
Tues /			
Wed /			
Thur /			
Fri /			

Comment

Date / /

READING AWARD

200 Nights

Worth planning a HOLIDAY or an ADVENTURE or a TRIP to celebrate your achievement for the year!

AWARDED TO

....

FOR
200 NIGHTS READING

Signed...

DATE: /   /

Date & Title	Comment	😊 😐 😟	Number of Days
Mon /			
Tues /			
Wed /			
Thur /			
Fri /			

Comment

Date / /

Date & Title	Comment	😊 😐 😟	Number of Days
Mon /			
Tues /			
Wed /			
Thur /			
Fri /			

Comment

Date / /

Date & Title	Comment	☺ ☺ ☹	Number of Days
Mon /			
Tues /			
Wed /			
Thur /			
Fri /			

Comment

Date / /

Date & Title	Comment		Number of Days
Mon /			
Tues /			
Wed /			
Thur /			
Fri /			

Comment

Date / /

Date & Title	Comment	😊 😐 😞	Number of Days
Mon /			
Tues /			
Wed /			
Thur /			
Fri /			
Comment			
		Date / /	
Mon /			
Tues /			
Wed /			
Thur /			
Fri /			
Comment			
		Date / /	

Reading Certificate

AWARDED TO

....

For Achieving

.... **Total Nights**

Reading for Year ....

Signed ....

Date & Title	Comment	😊 😐 ☹	Number of Days
Mon /			
Tues /			
Wed /			
Thur /			
Fri /			
Comment			
		Date / /	
Mon /			
Tues /			
Wed /			
Thur /			
Fri /			
Comment			
		Date / /	